ALL YOU NEED TO KNOW ABOUT BECOMING AN AMAZING ADVENTURER

How to Be an Explorer

Emma Lynch

Contents

Have You Got What It Takes?

EXPLORERS WANTED

Brave and bold explorers are needed to discover new things about our world. There will be excitement and challenges. There may even be danger too.

You will get to:

- travel the world and make incredible discoveries
- find places that no one has ever visited
- uncover lost worlds and people
- discover new plants, animals and sources of food.

All this and more awaits you in the opportunity of a lifetime.

Explorer Checklist

To become an explorer you will need to:

- ✔ learn how to cope in tough places and difficult situations
- ✔ be ready for extreme weather conditions
- ✔ pack the right things
- ✔ use maps and **GPS** (global positioning system) to guide you to places
- ✔ know how to find food, water, shelter and heat
- ✔ record information about what you find
- ✔ cope with sudden change, unexpected situations and emergencies.

It takes time and training to be an explorer. After all, it's a dangerous job, so you need to know what you're doing. Read on and maybe one day you will make discoveries of your very own.

Why Explore?

Starting Out

Being an explorer is a truly adventurous job. So what makes some people take on the challenge?

Exploration takes place at sea, as well as on land.

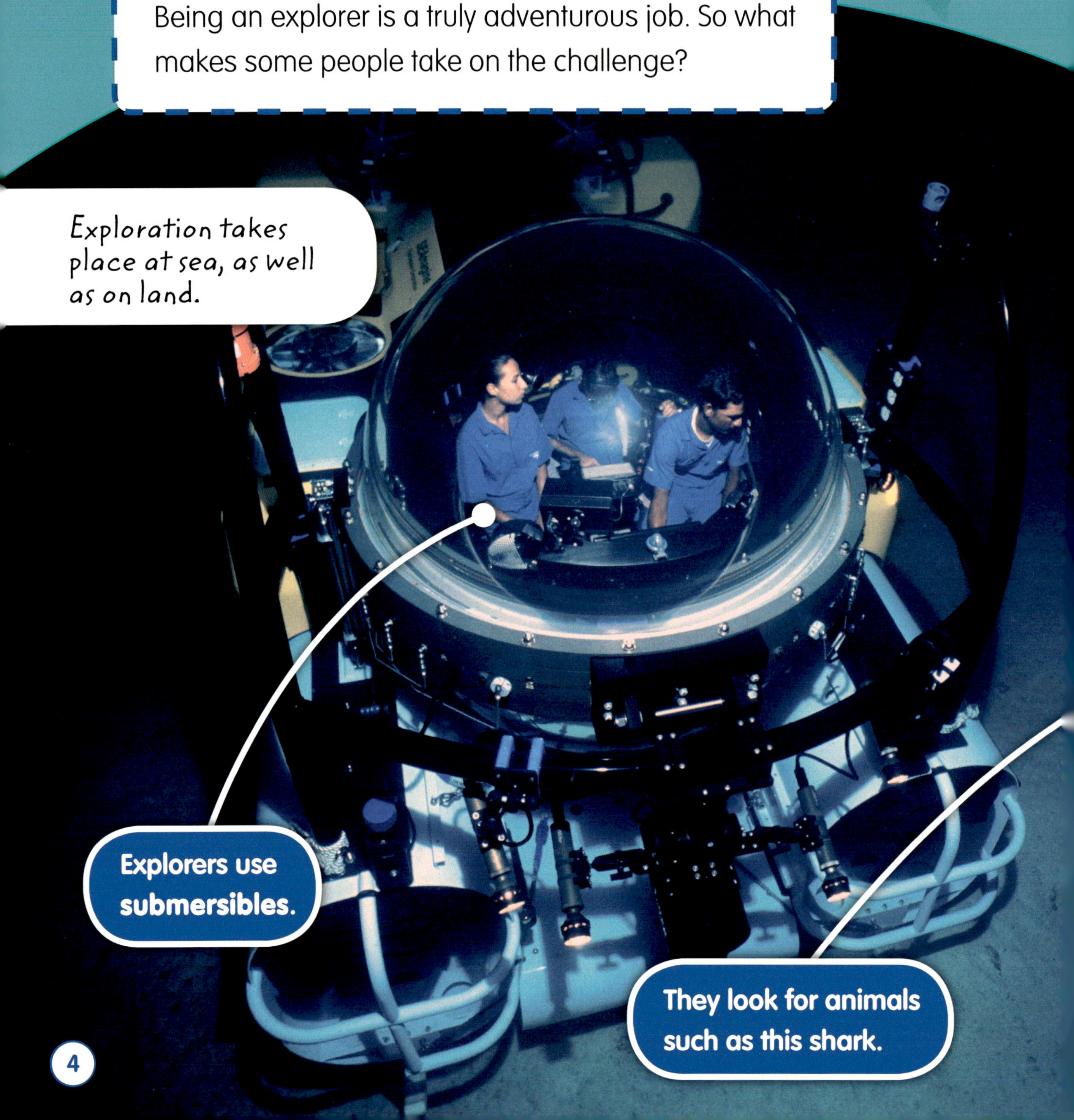

Explorers use submersibles.

They look for animals such as this shark.

New Challenges

For many people, being an explorer gives them the chance to discover new places, people, animals or plants. Other explorers want to help protect places that are in danger, such as rainforests. Some want to see how they cope in tough conditions, such as the extreme cold of Antarctica.

Name: Sir Edmund Hillary
Born/Died: 20 July 1919 – 11 January 2008
Country: New Zealand

Mount Everest is the highest mountain in the world and many people have died trying to reach the top. On 29 May 1953, Sir Edmund Hillary and Tenzing Norgay became the first climbers to reach the **summit**. Hillary said, "It is not the mountain we conquer, but ourselves."

Sir Edmund carried extra oxygen to help him breathe near the summit.

No Way!

Some of the deepest parts of the sea have not yet been fully explored.

Where in the World?

The Choice Is Yours

As an explorer, you get to visit some of the world's most amazing places and toughest **habitats**.

Deserts

Deserts are the world's dry places, but not all are covered with sand. Some are flat and stony, while others are rocky and hilly. Some are even covered in ice! Explorers go to deserts to study how animals and plants survive in such harsh and dry conditions.

Seas and Oceans

Oceans cover 71 per cent of Earth. The biggest oceans are the Pacific, the Atlantic and the Indian Oceans. Explorers discover new life in the oceans every year.

Polar Regions

Antarctica is a large land mass found at the South Pole. The Arctic is a huge area of ice around the North Pole. Explorers study the animals in the polar regions and the effects of **global warming**.

Tropical Rainforests

Tropical rainforests are found close to the **Equator**. The weather is warm and wet – perfect for plants. Explorers go to see the wide variety of animals and plants that live there.

Mountains

There are mountains all around the world. Some mountains stand alone and others are part of a "range" or group of mountains. Explorers enjoy the challenge of conquering mountain summits.

When to Go

Careful Planning

There are a lot of things explorers need to consider to make sure they travel at the best times.

Animals Travel Too

Before they set off, explorers searching for animals need to know where to find them each season. Some animals **migrate**, moving to warmer places when the weather gets cold and then returning when it gets warmer.

Wildebeest can migrate 2800 km in search of grass and water, so you need to know the best time of year to see them.

The Weather

Explorers often go to extreme habitats where the weather can make travel nearly impossible.

Winter at the North and South Poles is not very welcoming.

Travel in Southeast Asia is harder during the months of June – September because of **monsoon** rain.

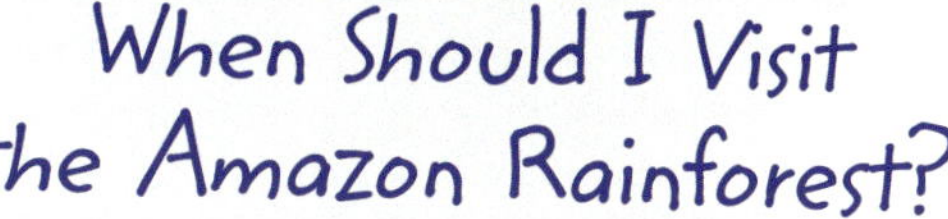

When Should I Visit the Amazon Rainforest?

December to March	June to October
This is the rainiest time. The rivers will be higher so I will be able to travel by canoe.	These are the drier months. I won't be able to travel as far by canoe.
I will be able to see animals by the river's edge.	It will be easier to track animals because the land will be dry.

The Amazon is the largest rainforest in the world. It has the highest number of animal species, too.

Pack Your Bags

Take the Right Things

Explorers pack different equipment and clothing for different places and different weather. However, there are some **essential** items that they must always pack for their safety and survival.

Your backpack should be comfortable to carry and large enough for your gear. Test it out on a few long walks before your trip.

Top Tip

Pack your backpack in reverse order, so that the things you need first will be at the top.

Essential Items

Matches that are kept dry can be used to make a fire.

A pocket-knife can be used to cut wood and food.

A compass and map can help you find your way. Also pack a handheld GPS.

A torch shows people where you are and helps you see in the dark.

A whistle can be used to signal for help.

Always carry a water bottle.

String or cord is useful for making shelters.

A fleece jacket will keep you warm and a waterproof coat will keep you dry.

Chocolate or high-energy snack bars are useful when you cannot find other food.

Pack your first-aid kit near the top so you can get to it quickly.

An explorer should also take:

- a camera
- a magnifying glass
- binoculars
- small bags to collect things
- a notebook and a pen.

Find Your Way

Which Way?

Imagine you are deep in a forest. There are trees all around you. Which way do you go? When there are no signs or roads to follow, explorers sometimes use a compass and a map to **navigate**.

North, South, East or West?

A compass can help you work out where you are. The compass arrow always points to the direction of north. From here you can see the positions of east, south and west, too. A good map will also show these positions.

On the map	Compass direction
Top	North (N)
Right	East (E)
Bottom	South (S)
Left	West (W)

Remember to keep your eyes open for clues when you are lost.

Some maps show the position of rivers, mountains, villages and railways.

Top Tip

A compass and a map can be lined up to guide you in the right direction.

How Far Is It?

Different maps are drawn to different scales. On one map, 1 cm might show 1 km, and on another map 1 cm could show 10 km. To work out the distance between two places, you need to know the scale of the map.

Many explorers use GPS to help them navigate. A GPS uses information from satellites to show exactly where you are on Earth, and how to get from where you are to where you want to be.

Try It!

Make a map for a friend to follow. Remember to show north, south, east and west.

SOS! Lost

Be Prepared

What would you do if you were lost and had no map, compass or GPS? Explorers would tell you to look for clues in the sky.

During the Day

The Sun always rises in the east and sets in the west. At midday in the southern **hemisphere**, the Sun points north. Explorers can use these markers like a compass.

Safety and the Sun

The Sun is an incredibly bright star. You must never look directly at it when using it to find your way.

At Night

Explorers use the Southern Cross constellation to find south at night. It never disappears below the horizon, which means it can always be seen.

Top Tip

Sometimes if you are lost it is best to stay where you are and wait to be rescued.

No Way!

People have used the stars to navigate for thousands of years.

Try It!

The Southern Cross is a constellation of five bright stars. To be sure you are looking at the Southern Cross, look for two bright stars nearby.

Set Up Camp

Choose the Right Spot

When explorers have reached their destination or if it is getting dark, they need to set up camp. They have to be careful though – they don't want any nasty surprises!

The toilet area should be away from the tent, food and water.

The fire should be away from trees, so it does not start a fire.

Set up camp near water – you will need it for cleaning, cooking and drinking.

Put up the tent in a sheltered spot away from strong winds.

Level ground is best. Avoid places that are rocky, on a steep slope, or where an animal has been sheltering – it might come back!

Build the fire close to your tent. It should keep you warm but not be dangerous.

No Way!

Bears have an amazing sense of smell. They can smell food from over 25 km away.

Food and rubbish attracts animals, such as bears, to campsites.

Set up camp quickly if bad weather is coming or night is falling.

Sometimes explorers have to camp in extreme places.

Top Tip

Be careful where you put your tent. You don't want to camp on an ant hill.

SOS! Take Shelter

Do-it-yourself Tent

Sometimes the worst happens and explorers have to survive without tents. They build emergency shelters out of any material they can find. Sometimes they even dig holes in the snow to shelter in.

Brigitte Muir is a mountaineer.

Name: Brigitte Muir

Born: 1958

Country: Australia

In 1997, Brigitte Muir became the first Australian woman to reach the summit of Mount Everest – but it took her three earlier attempts to do it. On one of these attempts, Brigitte became separated from her group at 2 a.m. She had to wait three hours until daylight before making her way back down the mountain. She nearly died of **hypothermia**.

A snow hole is a good way to shelter from the weather if you are lost in the snow.

Build a Shelter

Make sure your shelter faces away from the wind.

1 Find a strong branch to stand upright next to a tree.

2 Rest another branch between the top of the upright branch and the tree.

3 Lean long branches against the top branch and tie with string.

4 Add more branches as uprights at the sides and fasten with string.

5 Fill in the gaps with grass, bracken and large leaves.

Try It!

Try building your own emergency shelter next to a tree. Make sure your shelter is sturdy before you test it out!

Light a Fire

Make a Fire Bow Drill

Fire is an essential tool for survival. Explorers need fire to keep them warm, cook their food and keep away insects. Most explorers use matches to light fires, but there are other things they can use.

You can make a fire bow drill using dry wood and string.

1 The handhold holds the drill in place.

2 The bow is pushed back and forwards. This spins the drill.

3 The drill spins against the fireboard.

4 The rubbing movement produces heat. A tiny ember is made.

5 The ember is added to dried grass and twigs to start a fire.

6 Blowing the ember gently, helps the fire burn.

Be Fire Safe

Take great care when building and lighting fires. Remember:

- Do not light fires near trees and plants – they might catch fire.
- Do not light a fire in very dry, hot weather – it might spread and start a bushfire or grass fire.
- Children can help to build the fire, but only grown-ups should light fires.

No Way!

Explorers can also use magnifying glasses to start fires.

Without a fire, explorers would have to eat cold meals all the time.

SOS! Find Food and Drink

Which Food Is Safe?

Sometimes explorers run out of food and need to know how to survive in the wilderness. They need to know which wild foods are safe to eat, otherwise they could become very sick. They might even die.

Top Tip

Explorers are very experienced. It is not safe for anyone else to find food this way.

Wild Food

OK

- fruit
- herbs
- **SOME** berries and leaves (not all are safe)

Beware

- mushrooms – many are poisonous
- plants with thorns and spikes
- plants with shiny leaves – some are poisonous

The fruit and seeds from the native Australian quandong tree are safe to eat.

How to Trap Water

If explorers are a long way from a fresh water supply, they have to find ways of collecting water. One easy way is to trap the water that plants produce.

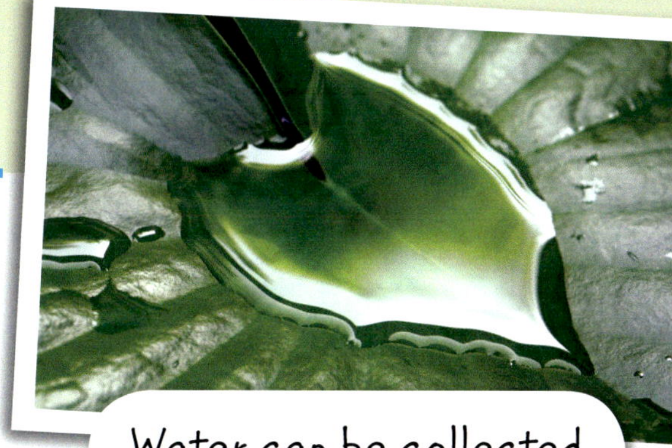

Water can be collected from leaves.

1 Tie a plastic bag over some leaves.

2 Wait for the Sun to shine on the leaves.

3 Water in the plant will **evaporate** from the leaves.

4 Wait for the water to form **condensation** inside the bag.

5 Collect the water and drink it.

No Way!

People can survive without food for about three weeks, but they can only survive for three days without water.

Go Exploring

Record It

Getting to a place is only part of the challenge. Explorers also collect information about plants, animals, people, places and weather. Sometimes they collect information using cameras, computers and sound-recording equipment. Sometimes, however, explorers just need to sit still and record what they see by sketching and writing.

An explorer studying an emperor penguin in Antarctica

No Way!

Explorers in Australia discovered this new species of jellyfish 1400 metres below sea level.

When you see something unusual, keep a note of the place, date and time.

Place: Kinabalu National Park, Malaysia

Date: 24 April 2011

Time: 11:03 a.m.

Record: Unusual plant found growing in moist soil at the bottom of Mount Kinabalu. Its stem is approximately 3 m long and runs along the ground. Its leaves are large and green. Reddish-purple pot-like traps grow from the stem. The traps are approximately 20 cm tall and 12 cm wide. Insects that fall into the traps are eaten by the plant.

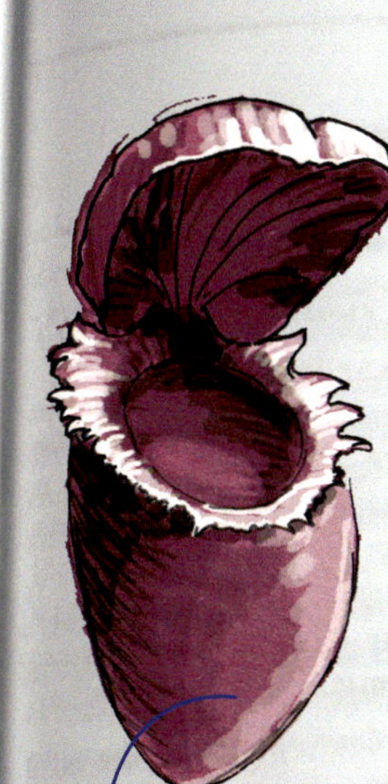

reddish purple pot-like trap

Try It!

You don't have to travel far to be an explorer. You can explore a local park, your garden or your school grounds. Keep an explorer's diary and record where you go and what you see.

Go Tracking

Seek the Signs

Most animals are afraid of people and keep away from them. Explorers track animals by looking carefully for signs. They look for:

- animal tracks
- crushed plants or dropped food
- hair and feathers caught on branches
- scat (animal poo).

Some animals leave claw marks in tree bark. Explorers look for clues like these koala scratches.

Animals often have regular travel routes and leave clues, such as footprints, along the way. These are kangaroo footprints.

Hamish does research in the polar regions.

Name: **Hamish Pritchard**
Born: **1 December 1974**
Country: **Britain**

When Hamish was working in the Arctic, he came across a polar bear. He stopped and watched the bear watch him. Eventually it wandered off. Later, however, the bear sneaked up on him! Hamish started up his **skidoo** and the noise scared the bear away. He didn't see the bear again, but Hamish knew it was still nearby when he saw a trail of giant footprints that followed his own tracks.

Top Tip

If you meet animals in the wild, keep your distance. Don't feed them or frighten them.

Polar bears usually eat seals, but anything they come across can be prey.

SOS! Emergency

First Aid

When you are in an extreme habitat, anything can happen. Explorers need a good knowledge of first aid before they set off.

Problem	First Aid
Insect bite or sting	Take out the sting. Cover with painkilling cream to soothe the itch.
Cuts	Clean the cut with an antiseptic wipe. Put an adhesive dressing on it.
Bruises	Place a cold, wet cloth on the bruise. Lift the limb with the bruise above the heart for 15 minutes. This reduces the size of the bruise.
Heat stroke (feeling dizzy, sick and weak with headache)	Move out of sunlight into a cool place. Undress and apply cool cloths. Lie down with feet higher than head. Drink lots of water.

These are some of the most common medical problems an explorer will face.

No Way!

Midges and mosquitoes hate Vitamin B1. Eat food such as nuts and rice to keep the bugs away!

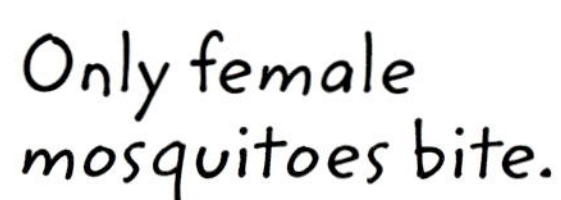

Only female mosquitoes bite.

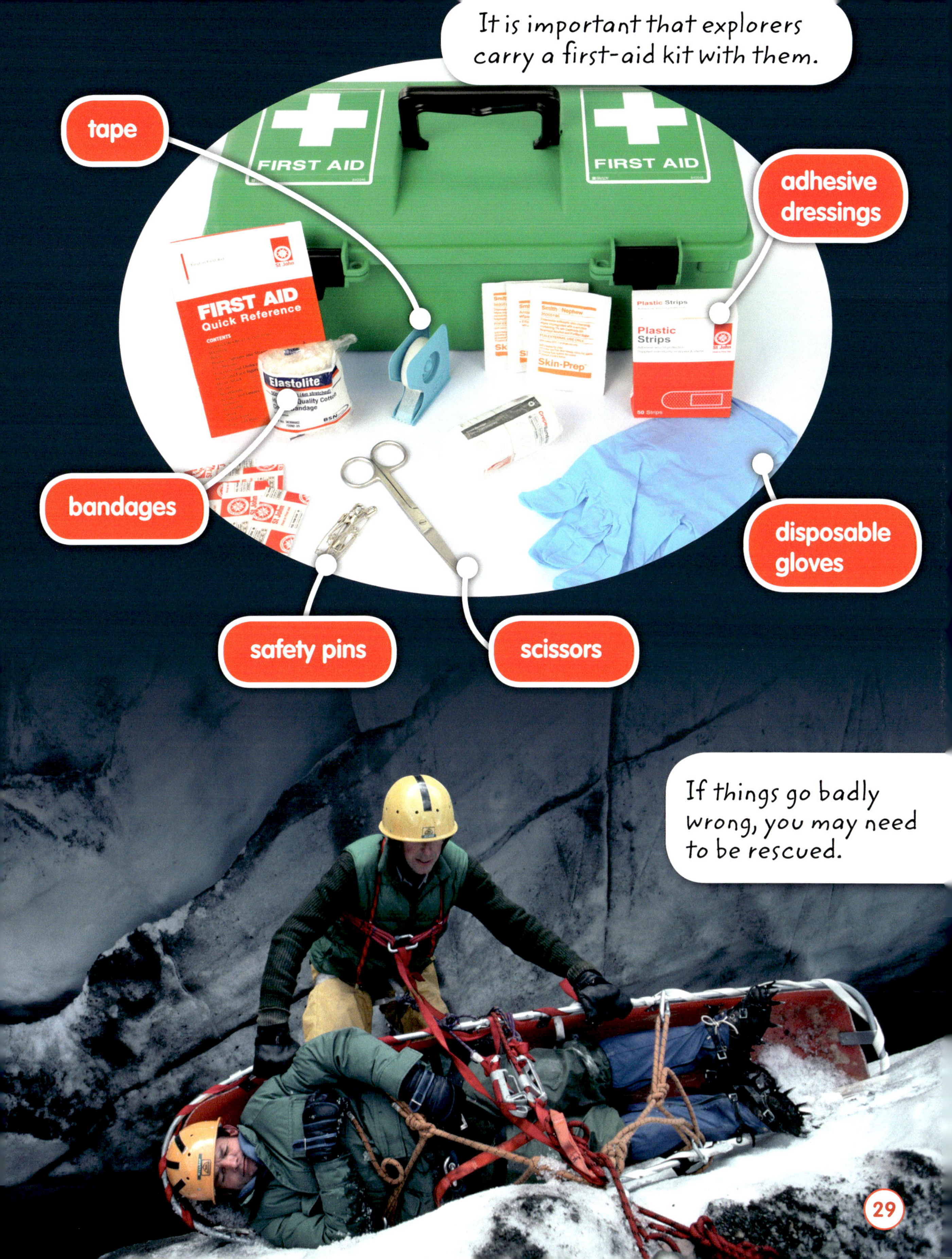
It is important that explorers carry a first-aid kit with them.
tape
adhesive dressings
bandages
disposable gloves
safety pins
scissors
FIRST AID
FIRST AID
FIRST AID Quick Reference
Elastolite
Plastic Strips
Skin-Prep
If things go badly wrong, you may need to be rescued.

Test Yourself

Do you think you have what it takes to be an explorer? Do this quiz to find out!

1

You are planning a trip. Do you:

A pack carefully, putting the things you will need first at the top of your backpack?

B pack the important things, but not in any order?

C pack lots of things into the largest backpack you can find?

2

You are lost. Do you:

A save your energy and wait to be rescued?

B try to find your way by the Sun and stars?

C keep going, hoping you will find the place soon?

3

You are exploring but it is getting dark. Do you:

A look for a flat spot to put up your tent?

B put the tent up where you are?

C continue exploring – there is more you want to see?

4

You see an animal. Do you:

A keep still and quietly watch it?

B move quietly towards it?

C move towards it and try to touch it?

5

You are exploring when you start to feel dizzy and sick. Do you:

A move to a cool place and drink lots of water?

B drink more water but keep going?

C keep going as there is no time to stop?

How did you do?

Mostly As
Congratulations, you are a born explorer!

Mostly Bs
Well done. You are on the right track, but there is more you could learn.

Mostly Cs
You have a lot to learn before you go out in the wilderness.

Glossary

condensation water that collects from the air on a cool surface

ember glowing, hot piece of wood or coal

Equator imaginary line around the middle of the Earth dividing it into North and South

essential necessary

evaporate when liquid turns to vapour

global warming harmful rise in the world's temperature

GPS system that uses satellites to find location or position

habitats places where certain animals or plants live

hemisphere one half of the planet as divided by the Equator

hypothermia when someone's body temperature falls below normal and they become ill

migrate move from one place to another and settle there

monsoon a rainy season

navigate find your way

skidoo sledge with an engine

submersibles vehicles that can explore under water, like a submarine

summit highest point

Index